Contents

OXFORD

UNIVERSITY PRESS

Great Clarendon Street, Oxford, OX2 6DP, United Kingdom

Oxford University Press is a department of the University of Oxford. It furthers the University's objective of excellence in research, scholarship, and education by publishing worldwide. Oxford is a registered trade mark of Oxford University Press in the UK and in certain other countries

This edition first published 2018

British Library Cataloguing in Publication Data
Data available

ISBN: 978-0-19-276481-2

10 9

Paper used in the production of this book is a natural, recyclable product made from wood grown in sustainable forests. The manufacturing process conforms to the environmental regulations of the country of origin.

Printed in China

Acknowledgements

Series Editor: Clare Kirtley

Cover illustration by Andy Hammond

The
Red Man
and the
Green Man

Tips for reading The Red Man and the Green Man together

This story practises these letter patterns:

> ee ea e y (all pronounced *ee* as in *three*)
>
> ie i-e igh i (all pronounced *ie* as in *tie*)
>
> oa ow o-e o (all pronounced *oe* as in *toe*)
>
> ai ay a-e a (all pronounced *ai* as in *train*)

Ask your child to point to these letter patterns and say the sounds (e.g. *ie* as in *cries*). Look out for these letter patterns in the story.

Your child might find these words tricky:

> of into to the are they all live people these says one two goes have some roll here do what

These words are common, but your child may not be able to sound them out yet. Say the words for your child if they do not know them.

Before you begin, ask your child to read the title. Remind your child to read words they do not recognise by sounding out first (saying each sound out loud, e.g. *gr-ee-n*) and then blending the word together (e.g. *green*). Look at the picture together. What do you think this story is about?

When you have finished reading the story, look through it again and:

- Ask your child, *Why didn't the red man and the green man enjoy their holiday?* (Because no one did what they told them to do.)
- Find and read some words on pages 19 and 20 that contain a long *ie* sound (*lights, seaside, right*). Point to the letter patterns that make the long *ie* vowel sound (*igh, i-consonant-e, igh*).

4

The red man and the green man live inside the traffic lights.

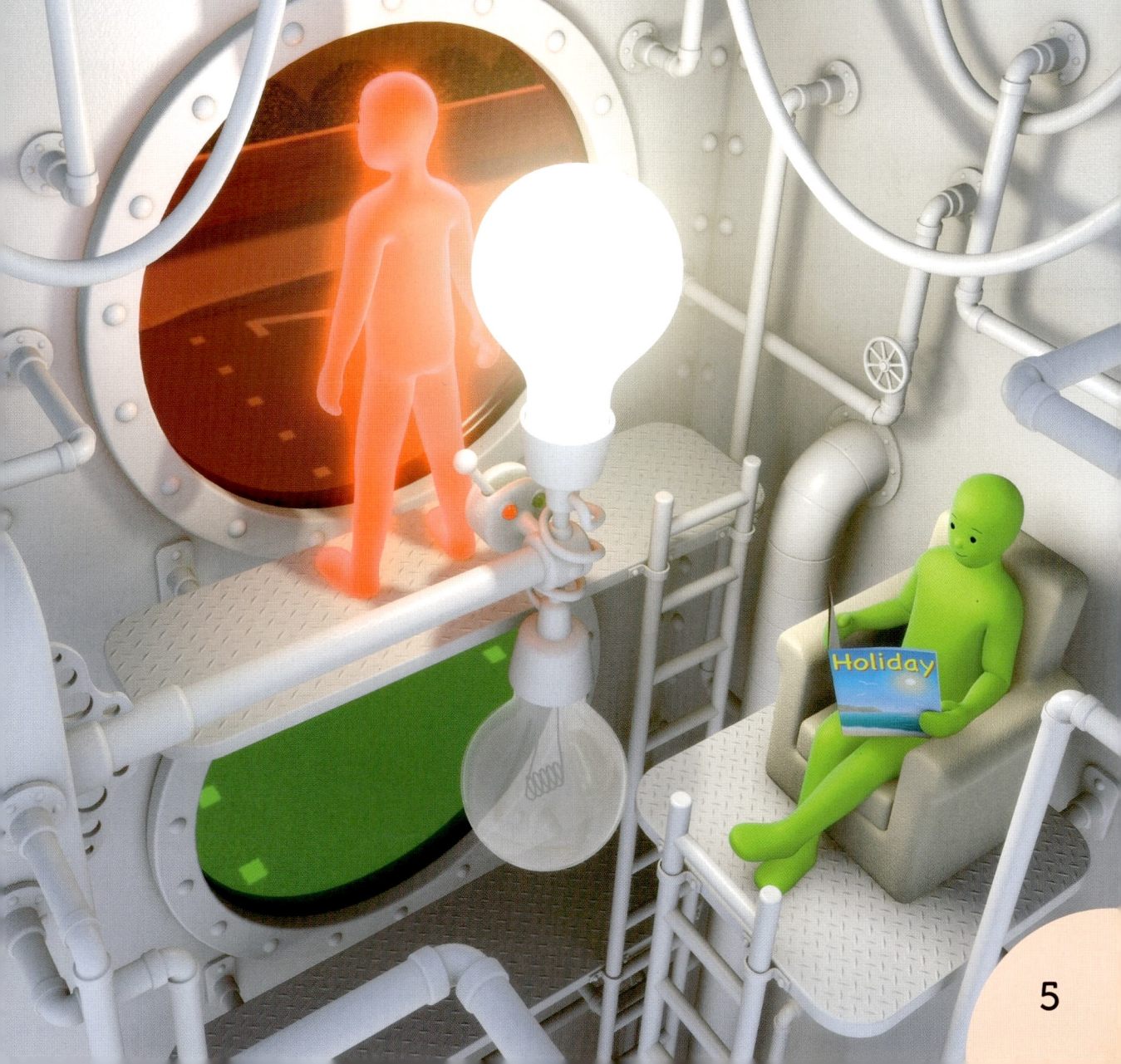

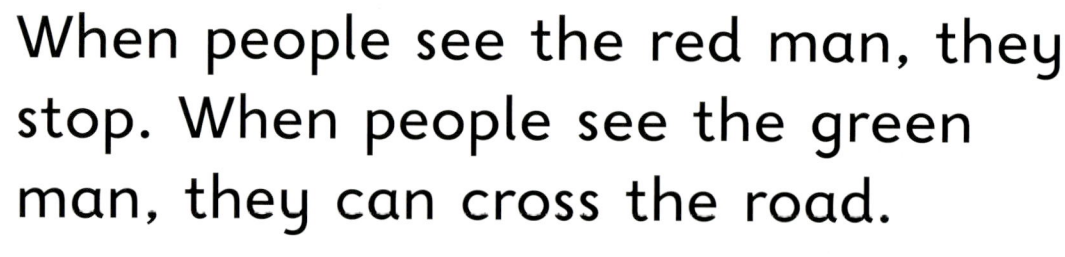

When people see the red man, they stop. When people see the green man, they can cross the road.

"I'm sick of these traffic lights," the red man says one day.
"So am I," says the green man.
"Let's go on holiday."

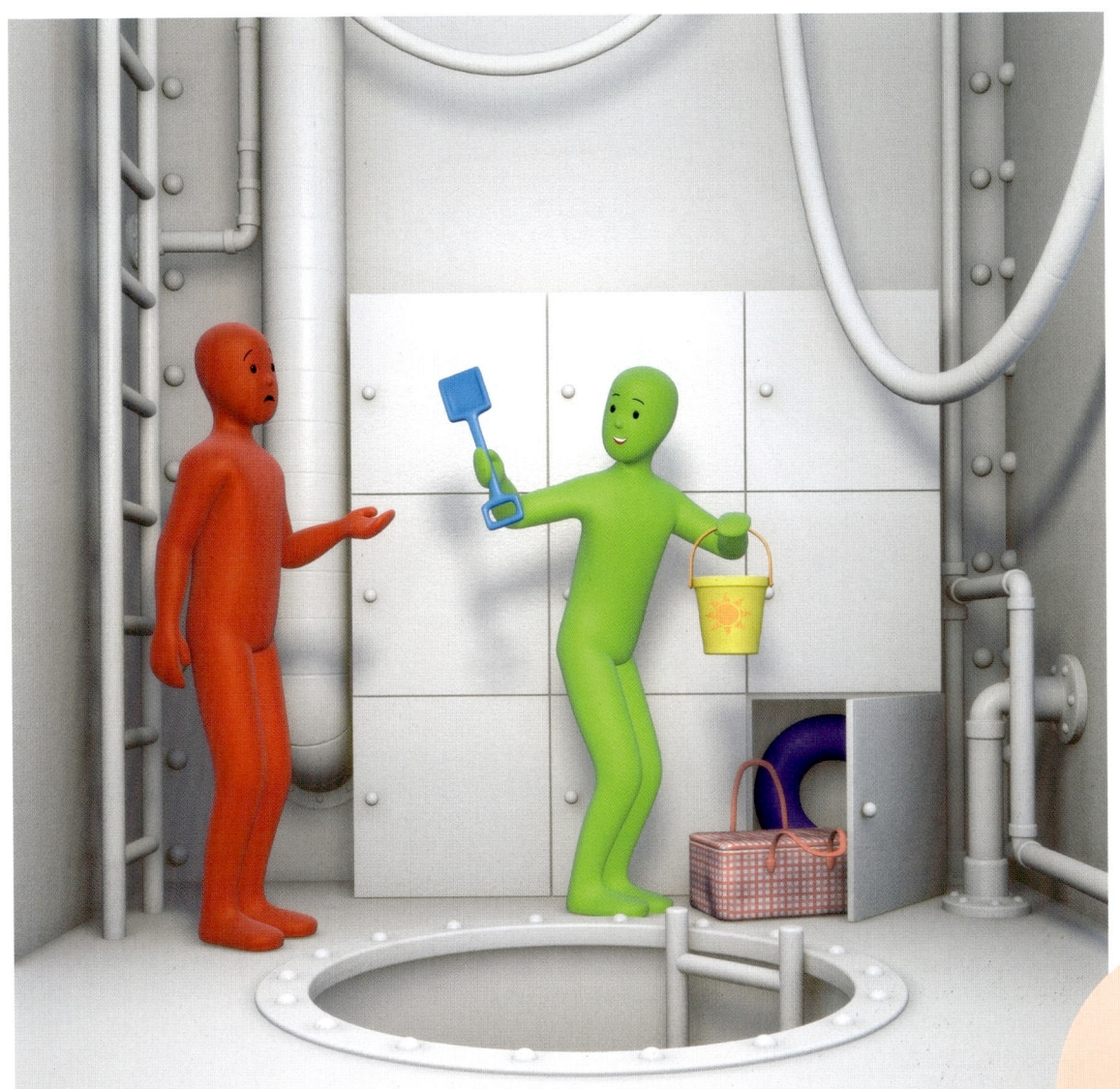

The red man and the green man get on a train. "Go, train, go," says the green man. But the train stays still.

In the end the train goes. The red man and the green man have a cup of tea.

The red man sees the sea. "Stop, train, stop!" he cries. But the train keeps going.

In the end the train stops. The red man and the green man get off.

11

The two men go to the beach.
They make some traffic lights in
the sand.

But then the waves roll in.
"Stop, waves, stop!" cries the red
man. But the waves don't stop.

They see a sea snail. It is sitting on a rock.

"Go, snail, go!" says the green man.
But the snail stays still.

Go, snail, go!

"No one stops when I tell them,"
says the red man.
"And no one goes when I tell
them," says the green man.
"Let's go home."

The red man and the green man go back on the train.

Back home, no one knows when to cross the road. They are happy to see the red man and the green man again.

The two men hop up into the traffic lights.

"The seaside is all right, but here people do what we tell them," they say.

Pirates

Tips for reading Pirates together

This story practises these letter patterns:

> ee ea e y (all pronounced *ee* as in *three*)
>
> ie i-e igh i y (all pronounced *ie* as in *tie*)
>
> oa ow o-e o (all pronounced *oe* as in *toe*)
>
> ai ay a-e a (all pronounced *ai* as in *train*)

Ask your child to point to these letter patterns and say the sounds (e.g. *y* as in *shy*). Look out for these letter patterns in the story.

Your child might find these words tricky:

> to the of you they for pirate comes have
> we've want

These words are common, but your child may not be able to sound them out yet. Say the words for your child if they do not know them.

Before you begin, ask your child to read the title. Remind your child to read words they do not recognise by sounding out first (saying each sound out loud, e.g. *J-a-ck*) and then blending the word together (e.g. *Jack*). Look at the picture together. What do you think this story is about?

When you have finished reading the story, look through it again and:

- Ask your child, *Why didn't Jack and Jade fight?* (They were too hot, then too hungry. Finally they became friends.)
- Find and read some words on page 37 that contain a long *ie* sound (*shy, I, write, I'll*). Point to the letter patterns that make the long vowel sound (*y, i, i-consonant-e, I*). Find and read some words on page 38 that contain a long *ai* sound (*Jade, wave, they, sail, away*).

Jack is a pirate. He is digging for gold.

Jack digs a deep hole.

While Jack is asleep, along comes
Pirate Jade.

Jade begins to dig in Jack's hole.

She digs up a chest and opens the lid.

Jack wakes up and sees Jade.

29

Jack and Jade have a swim. They splash and play.

31

Jade catches a fish and Jack lights a fire.

Then they eat lunch.

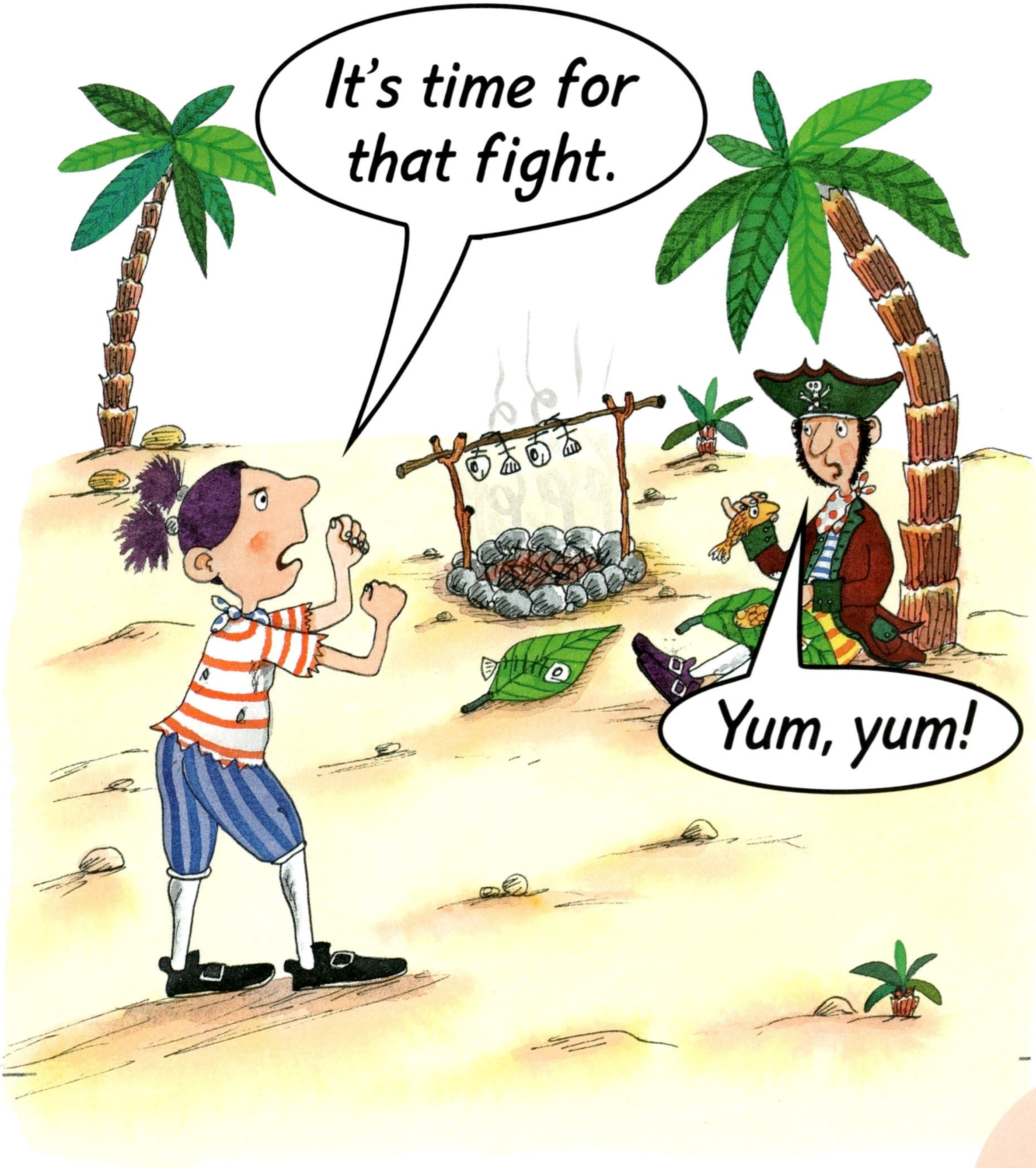
It's time for that fight.
Yum, yum!

34

35

Jack and Jade load their boats.
Then it's time to go.

Jack feels shy.

Jack and Jade wave as they sail away.

Tails

Tips for reading Tails together

This story practises these letter patterns:

ee ea e y (all pronounced *ee* as in *three*)

ie i-e y i (all pronounced *ie* as in *tie*)

ow o (pronounced *oe* as in *toe*)

ai ay a-e a (all pronounced *ai* as in *train*)

Ask your child to point to these letter patterns and say the sounds (e.g. *ee* as in *three*). Look out for these letter patterns in the story.

Your child might find these words tricky:

the to of you all her have do wants

These words are common, but your child may not be able to sound them out yet. Say the words for your child if they do not know them.

Before you begin, ask your child to read the title. Remind your child to read words they do not recognise by sounding out first (saying each sound out loud, e.g. *t-ai-l-s*) and then blending the word together (e.g. *tails*). Look at the picture together. What do you think this story is about?

When you have finished reading the story, look through it again and:

- Ask your child, *Are tails useful?* (Yes, animals use them in lots of ways: to signal; to help them jump; to help them swim; to help them catch their food; to swish away flies; to show off!)

- Find and read some words on pages 43, 44 and 45 that contain a long *ee* sound (*She, sees, puppy, stumpy, He, happy*). Point to the letter patterns that make the long vowel sound (*e, ee, y, y, e, y*).

Lots of animals have tails.
Tails can be all shapes and sizes.

a zebra's tail

a rat's tail

a whale's tail

a goat's tail

a lion's tail

a crocodile's tail

a skunk's tail

41

This cat has a long black tail.
She waves it when she is cross.

She fluffs it up when she sees a dog.

This kitten likes to chase its tail.

This puppy has a stumpy tail.
He wags it when he is happy.

This rabbit has a white bobtail.
It flashes when he runs.

That is a signal to run away.

This squirrel has a tail like a brush.
It helps him leap.

This fox has a brush as well. So do her three cubs.

49

Fish have tails which help them to swim.

This stingray stings fishes with its tail. Then it eats them.

Snakes have scaly tails.

This snake kills the animals it is going to eat, by crushing them.

This pony has a tail which can swish away flies.

This peacock has an amazing tail. He opens it up like a fan when he wants to show off.

I wish I had a tail!

Pen-Pals

Tips for reading Pen-Pals together

This story practises these letter patterns:

> ee   ea   e   y   (all pronounced *ee* as in *three*)
> ie   i-e   igh   i   (all pronounced *ie* as in *tie*)
> oa   o-e   o   (all pronounced *oe* as in *toe*)
> ai   ay   a-e   a   (all pronounced *ai* as in *train*)

Ask your child to point to these letter patterns and say the sounds (e.g. *o-e* as in *jokes*). Look out for these letter patterns in the story.

Your child might find these words tricky:

> of   the   to   you   your   was   are   school   have   one
> do   come   love   sneeze   today   can't   goes

These words are common, but your child may not be able to sound them out yet. Say the words for your child if they do not know them.

Before you begin, ask your child to read the title. Remind your child to read words they do not recognise by sounding out first (saying each letter out loud, e.g. *p-e-n*) and then blending the word together (e.g. *pen*). Look at the picture together. What do you think this story is about?

When you have finished reading the story, look through it again and:

- Ask your child, *Did Joan enjoy her stay with Megan? How do you know?* (Yes, because she wrote to Megan that she had had a fab time.)
- Find and read some words on page 71 that contain a long *oe* sound (*Joan, crocodile, home, told, jokes*). Point to the letter patterns that make the long *oe* vowel sound (*oa, o, o-consonant-e, o, o-consonant-e*).

Hi Megan

I am your American pen-pal. My name is Joan and I am nine. Next May, twenty kids from my school will be visiting the UK. Can I stay with you?

Best wishes, Joan

Hi Joan

I am glad we are pen-pals. Yes, you can stay with us in May. I am nine as well, and I like animals. I have a dog. His name is Rex. Have you got a pet?

Best wishes, Megan

Hi Megan

No, I don't have a pet. Dogs make me sneeze. I like playing tennis. I hope you like tennis too.

Joan

Hi Joan
I'm afraid I don't play tennis. I read
a lot. Do you like reading?
Megan

Hi Megan

I don't read much but I like TV. My plane gets in at eleven on Friday. Will you meet me?

I hope we will get on.

Joan

Hi Joan

Yes, we can meet the plane. Sorry but we don't have a TV. We did have one but it got broken.

See you on Friday!

Megan

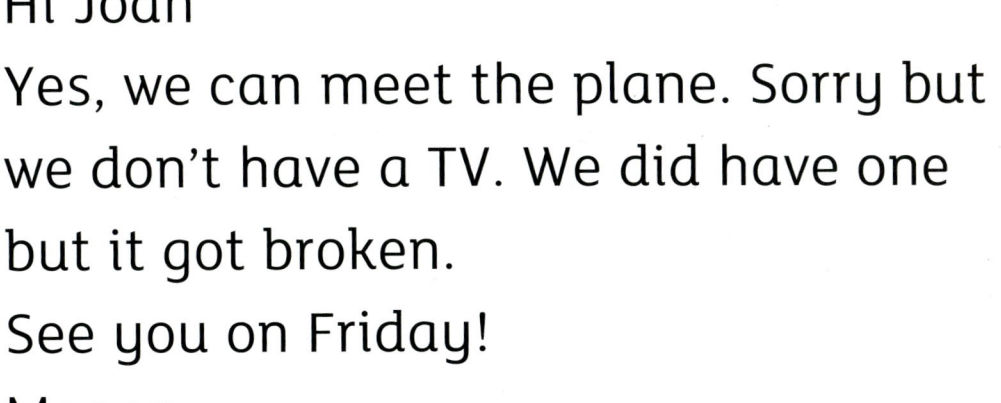

May 1

We met Joan's plane. She is very quiet. I think she is shy.

Rex made Joan sneeze. He had to go and stay with Granny.

Joan was sad today. I think she is missing home.

May 4

I went swimming with Joan.
It was fun.

May 5

Joan can play Dad's drums! We sang lots of songs. I like Joan a lot.

May 6

We went swimming again. Joan made up a game. I was a fish and she was a crocodile. Back home, we told lots of jokes.

May 7

Joan and I had a midnight feast!
I will be sad when she goes.

May 8

Joan had to go home. We got Rex back from Granny's, but I am missing Joan.

Hi Megan

I got home safely. I had such a fab time with you. I can't wait until you come and stay with me next May!

Lots of love

Joan

My Cat

Tips for reading My Cat together

This story practises these letter patterns:

> ee ea e y (all pronounced *ee* as in *three*)
> ie i-e igh i (all pronounced *ie* as in *tie*)
> ow o-e o (all pronounced *oe* as in *toe*)
> ai ay a-e a (all pronounced *ai* as in *train*)

Ask your child to point to these letter patterns and say the sounds (e.g. *ai* as in *tail*). Look out for these letter patterns in the story.

Your child might find these words tricky:

> to of the out about you head can't

These words are common, but your child may not be able to sound them out yet. Say the words for your child if they do not know them.

Before you begin, ask your child to read the title. Remind your child to read words they do not recognise by sounding out first (saying each letter together, e.g. *c-a-t*) and then blending the word together (e.g. *cat*). Look at the picture together. What do you think this story is about?

When you have finished reading the story, look through it again and:

- Ask your child, *Why did the girl find it difficult to write a poem?* (The cat kept disturbing her.)
- Find and read two words that rhyme on pages 84 and 85 (*whale, tail*). Point to the letter pattern that makes the long vowel sound in these words (*a-consonant-e, ai*). Find and read some more words in the story that contain a long *ai* sound (*a, again, say, stay*).

I'm going to write a poem.
I find a pot of ink.
I find a pen. I find a pad.
I scratch my head and think.

I try to write a poem about my mum and dad.

But then the cat jumps on the desk and sits upon my pad.

I try to write a poem about the sea and sand.

But then the cat jumps up and knocks the pen out of my hand.

I try to write a poem
about a bright red rose.

But then the cat jumps up again
and licks me on the nose.

I know! I'll write a poem about a humpback whale.

This time the cat jumps up and knocks the ink off with his tail.

That silly cat keeps bugging me!
I pick him up and say,

"If you won't let me write my poem, then I won't let you stay."

The cat sits on the window sill.
He looks so cold and sad.

I try to write my poem
but I can't help feeling bad.

I suck my pen. I scratch my head.
I think of this and that.

Then suddenly
I've got it!
"I'll write about..."

"My cat!"

Tim's Bad Mood

Tips for reading Tim's Bad Mood together

This story practises this letter pattern:

oo

Ask your child to point to this letter pattern and say the sound
(e.g. *oo* as in *mood*). Look out for this letter pattern in the story.

Your child might find these words tricky:

the   are   said

These words are common, but your child may not be able to sound
them out yet. Say the words for your child if they do not know them.

Before you begin, ask your child to read the title. Remind your child
to read words they do not recognise by sounding out first (saying each
sound out loud, e.g. *m-oo-d*) and then blending the word together
(e.g. *mood*). Look at the picture together. What do you think this
story is about?

When you have finished reading the story, look through it again and:

- Ask your child, *Was the meat really too dry? How do you know?*
  (No, Tim was just grumpy about everything because he woke up
  in a bad mood.)
- Find and read some words with the long vowel sound *oo* on page
  98 (*spoon, too, stool*). Point to the letter pattern that makes the long
  vowel sound in these words. Find and read some more words in the
  story that contain the letter pattern *oo* (*mood, bedroom, food, boots,
  pool*). Try and write some on a piece of paper.

Tim Tomkins woke up in a very
bad mood.

Then Mum, Dad and Molly said...

Sue Kangaroo

Tips for reading Sue Kangaroo together

This story practises these letter patterns:

oo ew ue o (all pronounced *ue* as in *blue*)

Split vowels: a–e i–e o–e u–e

Ask your child to point to these letter patterns and say the sounds
(e.g. *oo* as in *kangaroo*). Look out for these letter patterns in the story.

Your child might find these words tricky:

can't dinner her here out Mrs says some
teacher the there tomorrow what your

These words are common, but your child may not have learned how
to sound them out yet. Say the words for your child if they do not
know them.

Before you begin, ask your child to read the title. Remind your child
to read words they do not recognise by sounding out first (saying
each sound out loud, e.g. *th-i-s*) and then blending the word together
(e.g. *this*). Look at the picture together. What do you think this story
is about?

- Ask your child, *Did Sue like school? How do you know?* (Yes,
  because she says 'Hooray' when she finds out that there is school
  tomorrow too.)

- On pages 128 and 129 find some words that rhyme (*Sue, glue, too*).
  Point to the letter pattern that makes the long *ue* sound in the
  words (*ue, oo*). On page 130 find more words that contain a long *ue*
  sound (*school, rules, Drew*). Point to the letter pattern that makes
  the long *ue* sound in each word (*oo, u–consonant–e, ew*).

This is school

and this is Sue

and this is
Mummy Kangaroo.

The teacher's name is Mrs Drew.

Sue   Prue   Luke

She says hello to Mum and Sue.

"This is Sue," says Mrs Drew.

"Do be kind to her. She's new."

"Time to paint," says Mrs Drew.

Sue says, "I like red and blue."

"Time to glue," says Mrs Drew.

"Sue can glue a kangaroo!"

"Dinner time," says Mrs Drew.

"This is yummy stew," says Sue.

"Music time," says Mrs Drew.

"I can play the spoons!" says Sue.

"Home time soon," says Mrs Drew.

"But what is in your pocket, Sue?"

Sue takes out a tube of glue.

She takes some spoons and
paint out too.

"The school has rules," says Mrs Drew.

"You can't take those things home with you."

Sue is sad. "Don't cry," says Prue.

"Play with them tomorrow, Sue."

"Is there school tomorrow too?"

"Is that true? Hooray!" says Sue.

Here is Mummy Kangaroo.
"Hi, Mum! School is cool!" says Sue.